12043

Team Spirit

THE BOSTON CELTICS

BY

MARK STEWART

Content Consultant
Matt Zeysing
Historian and Archivist
The Naismith Memorial Basketball Hall of Fame

CHICAGO, ILLINOIS

Norwood House Press
P.O. Box 316598
Chicago, Illinois 60631

For information regarding Norwood House Press, please visit our website at:
www.norwoodhousepress.com or call 866-565-2900.

All photos courtesy of Getty Images except the following:
Capital Cards (6), TCMA, Inc. (14, 34 left), Dell Publishing Co. (20, 28),
Topps, Inc. (21, 26, 34 right, 35 top right & bottom left, 37, 41 both, 43),
Black Book Partners Archives (22, 27, 40), Complete Sports Publications, Inc. (35 top left),
Prentice-Hall, Inc. (36), Matt Richman (48).
Cover Photo: Elsa/Getty Images
Special thanks to Topps, Inc.

Editor: Mike Kennedy
Designer: Ron Jaffe
Project Management: Black Book Partners, LLC.
Research: Joshua Zaffos

Library of Congress Cataloging-in-Publication Data

Stewart, Mark, 1960-
    The Boston Celtics / by Mark Stewart ; content consultant, Matt Zeysing.
        p. cm. -- (Team spirit)
    Includes bibliographical references and index.
    Summary: "Presents the history and accomplishments of the Boston Celtics
basketball team. Includes highlights of players, coaches, and awards,
quotes, timelines, maps, glossary and websites"--Provided by publisher.
    ISBN-13: 978-1-59953-282-0 (library edition : alk. paper)
    ISBN-10: 1-59953-282-4 (library edition : alk. paper) 1. Boston Celtics
(Basketball team)--History--Juvenile literature. I. Zeysing, Matt. II.
Title.
    GV885.52.B67L43 2007
    796.323'640974461--dc22
                                                    2008039803

COVER PHOTO: The Celtics celebrate a win during the 2007–08 season.

Table of Contents

CHAPTER	PAGE
Meet the Celtics	4
Way Back When	6
The Team Today	10
Home Court	12
Dressed For Success	14
We Won!	16
Go-To Guys	20
On the Sidelines	24
One Great Day	26
Legend Has It	28
It Really Happened	30
Team Spirit	32
Timeline	34
Fun Facts	36
Talking Hoops	38
For the Record	40
Pinpoints	42
Play Ball	44
Glossary	46
Places to Go	47
Index	48

SPORTS WORDS & VOCABULARY WORDS: In this book, you will find many words that are new to you. You may also see familiar words used in new ways. The glossary on page 46 gives the meanings of basketball words, as well as "everyday" words that have special basketball meanings. These words appear in **bold type** throughout the book. The glossary on page 47 gives the meanings of vocabulary words that are not related to basketball. They appear in ***bold italic type*** throughout the book.

BASKETBALL SEASONS: Because each basketball season begins late in one year and ends early in the next, seasons are not named after years. Instead, they are written out as two years separated by a dash, for example 1944–45 or 2005–06.

Meet the Celtics

The official colors of the **National Basketball Association (NBA)** are red, white, and blue. Or are they green and white? Those are the colors of the Boston Celtics. For much of the last 50 years, the Celtics have shown how teamwork and team spirit can lead to success in the NBA.

The Celtics have won the NBA crown during five different *decades*—in the 1950s, 1960s, 1970s, 1980s, and in the 21st *century*. They have more championship banners hanging in their arena than any other team. Every Celtic can look up and understand that he is a part of basketball history.

This book tells the story of the Celtics. They are a proud team with a long *tradition* of excellence. Many times, this made the difference between victory and defeat. The Celtics win because their good players have the confidence to do great things—and because their great players always play for the good of the team.

Ray Allen, Kevin Garnett, James Posey, and Paul Pierce proudly display the trophy for Boston's 2007–08 NBA Championship.

Way Back When

Back in the 1930s and 1940s, **professional** basketball was not a popular sport. Teams played their games in tiny gyms in front of small crowds. The big arenas in cities such as New York and Boston usually held ice hockey games and college basketball games. In 1946, things began to change. The owners of big arenas decided professional basketball might be a smart way to make money when their buildings were not in use. They started a league that later became the NBA.

The leader of that group of owners was Walter Brown. He also oversaw the Boston Garden. Brown named his basketball team the Celtics, and then watched as his club struggled to win. The Celtics turned things around in the 1950–51 season. That is when Red Auerbach became their coach and Bob Cousy and Ed Macauley joined the team. Auerbach believed in a **fast break** attack on offense. Cousy was the NBA's best dribbler and passer. Macauley was one of the quickest centers in the league.

In 1956, the Celtics traded for a young center named Bill Russell. He was a *ferocious* defensive player and a great rebounder—and perfect for Auerbach's *system*. With Russell grabbing loose balls and Cousy leading the charge on offense, Boston scored lots of easy baskets. The team's top shooters included Bill Sharman, Tom Heinsohn, Frank Ramsey, Bailey

Howell, and Sam Jones. In 13 seasons from 1956–57 to 1968–69, the Celtics won the NBA Championship 11 times!

During the 1970s, a new group of Celtics took over. They were led by **All-Stars** John Havlicek and Dave Cowens. Havlicek was a crafty forward who had been a young star for Boston in the 1960s. He taught the next *generation* of Celtics how to play winning basketball. Havlicek teamed up with Cowens, Jo Jo White, and Paul Silas to form the heart of a club that won the NBA Championship in 1974 and 1976.

LEFT: A postcard of Red Auerbach, the greatest coach in team history.
ABOVE: Bob Cousy, Bill Russell, and Tom Heinsohn pose for a picture at the 1963 All-Star Game.

The Celtics were champions again in the 1980s. The team reached the **NBA Finals** five times and won three league titles. Boston's star player was a smart and talented forward named Larry Bird. Time and again, he made the winning play for the Celtics. Bird's teammates included Kevin McHale and Robert Parish. They played their best when they were close to the basket. Boston's "Big Three" got plenty of help from **role players** such as Nate Archibald, Cedric Maxwell, Gerald Henderson, Dennis Johnson, Bill Walton, M.L. Carr, and Danny Ainge.

After 40 years of winning, the Celtics began to struggle in the 1990s. The team hoped that top **draft picks** Len Bias and Reggie Lewis would become club leaders. Unfortunately, both died at a young age. Boston could not find new stars to replace them.

Eight years of losing finally came to an end in 2001–02. The Celtics welcomed a new group of talented young players that included Antoine Walker and Paul Pierce. The Celtics and their fans entered the 21st century hoping to add to the 16 championship banners hanging over their court.

LEFT: Larry Bird shoots over his friend and rival, Magic Johnson. Bird led the Celtics to three titles during the 1980s. **ABOVE**: Reggie Lewis looks for an opening in the defense.

The Team Today

Winning a 17th NBA Championship was not an easy task. The Celtics reached the **Eastern Conference Finals** in 2002 and the **conference semifinals** in 2003. Both times they lost to the New Jersey Nets. Boston fans grew angry after these disappointments. The team thought about starting all over again.

The Celtics traded Antoine Walker but kept Paul Pierce. They asked their young star to be patient while they rebuilt around him. It was not easy at times. In 2007–08, Pierce got the help he needed. The Celtics added Kevin Garnett, Ray Allen, and other experienced stars to the **roster**.

Just as in Boston's glory years, the **veterans** set the example for the young players. The Celtics returned to the NBA Finals and beat the Los Angeles Lakers. It was like the old days. The fans were excited again. As in years past, a new generation of winning players had stepped in to carry on the team's championship spirit.

Paul Pierce, Ray Allen, and Kevin Garnett get ready to dig in on defense during a 2007–08 game. They teamed up to guide Boston to its 17th NBA Championship.

Home Court

For 50 seasons, the Celtics played in the Boston Garden. It was America's most famous basketball court. The steep-sloping stands made the fans feel as if they were part of the action. The championship banners and jerseys hanging from the rafters reminded them of the organization's great teams and players.

Nothing in the Boston Garden was more recognizable than the parquet floor. The square-patterned court was unlike any other in the NBA. It included the Celtics *logo* at halfcourt.

In 1995, the Celtics moved into a "new" Garden. They took as much with them as they could—including the banners, jerseys, and of course the parquet floor. Both arenas were built over Boston's North Station. Today, it is still easy for fans to jump on a train and get to games from almost anywhere.

BY THE NUMBERS

- *There are 18,624 seats for basketball at the Celtics' arena.*
- *The arena took 27 months to build.*
- *The cost of construction in 1995 was $160 million.*

Boston's championship banners hang from the rafters of the Celtics' arena as fans celebrate the team's 2008 title.

Dressed for Success

The Celtics uniform has changed little over the years. For more than 60 seasons, the team has worn white with green trim at home, and green with white trim on the road. The home uniform has *Celtics* written across the front. The word *Boston* appears on their road uniforms.

The biggest change has been to the sneakers worn by the players. From their early days through the 1970s, they played in black sneakers.

During the 1980s, Boston switched to green. In recent years, the players have started wearing white sneakers.

The team's logo is one of the most famous in sports. It shows a leprechaun, which is a make-believe character from Irish legends. The first logo was drawn by Zang Auerbach, Red Auerbach's brother. At times, the Celtics have also used a shamrock as a team *symbol*.

Bill Sharman models the team's green uniform—and black sneakers—from the 1950s.

UNIFORM BASICS

The basketball uniform is very simple. It consists of a roomy top and baggy shorts.

- The top hangs from the shoulders, with big "scoops" for the arms and neck. This style has not changed much over the years.

- Shorts, however, have changed a lot. They used to be very short, so players could move their legs freely. In the last 20 years, shorts have actually gotten longer and much baggier.

Basketball uniforms look the same as they did long ago … until you look very closely. In the old days, the shorts had belts and buckles. The tops were made of a thick cotton called "jersey," which got very heavy when players sweated. Later, uniforms were made of shiny *satin*. They may have looked great, but they did not "breathe." Players got very hot! Today, most uniforms are made of *synthetic* materials that soak up sweat and keep the body cool.

Ray Allen makes a move to the basket in Boston's 2007–08 home uniform.

We Won!

During the early 1950s, the Celtics had the building blocks of a title contender. Bob Cousy, Bill Sharman, Tom Heinsohn, Frank Ramsey, Jim Loscutoff, and Andy Phillip were all top players. However, the Celtics did not become a championship team until Bill Russell joined them for the 1956–57 season. Coach Red Auerbach saw great *potential* in his rookie center. Russell blocked shots, hauled down rebounds, and fired long passes that led to easy baskets. He made his teammates even better.

The Celtics faced the St. Louis Hawks in the NBA Finals that spring. The series was not decided until Game 7. The Celtics and

Bob Cousy sneaks a pass by two defenders for the Los Angeles Lakers during the 1962 NBA Finals.

Hawks played two thrilling **overtimes** before Boston won 125–123. The Hawks got revenge by winning the 1958 NBA Finals. After that, however, the Celtics were unbeatable. Boston won the NBA Championship eight years in a row. Five of those victories came against the Los Angeles Lakers.

Only once during those eight championship seasons were the Celtics seriously challenged in the NBA Finals. In 1962, they trailed the Lakers after five games. Boston won Game 6 easily, but nearly lost Game 7. The Lakers missed a shot at the buzzer, and the game went into overtime. The Celtics pulled together and won 110–107.

The last two championships of the 1960s were the sweetest for the Celtics. In 1967–68 and 1968–69, many of Boston's players looked old and tired. They did not finish in first place in the Eastern Conference either season. But once the **playoffs** began, they came alive. Russell, now a **player-coach**, guided his teammates to victory over the Lakers in the NBA Finals both times.

John Havlicek and Dave Cowens led the Celtics to their next championship in 1974. They played like **Hall of Famers** in Game 7 against Kareem Abdul-Jabbar and the Milwaukee Bucks. Two years later, Jo Jo White was the star when Boston won its 13th NBA title, this time against the Phoenix Suns. One of the games in that series went into triple-overtime. Many say it was the most exciting contest ever played in the NBA Finals.

During the 1980s, the Celtics won three more championships with their "Big Three" of Larry Bird, Kevin McHale, and Robert Parish. They were able to shine because of their talented teammates. Players such as Cedric Maxwell—who was named **Most Valuable Player (MVP)** of the 1981 NBA Finals—carried on the team's great tradition of role players performing like superstars when the pressure was greatest. Boston beat the Houston Rockets in 1980–81 and 1985–86, and the Lakers in 1983–84.

The series with Los Angeles was one of the most thrilling ever. It featured basketball's best *rivalry*, between Bird and Magic Johnson. These two stars joined the NBA at a time when many people were losing interest in basketball. They made the Celtics and Lakers great again, and captured the imagination of millions of new fans.

Celtics fans got very used to winning. They never imagined they would have to wait 22 years for another championship. Many of the fans who watched Paul Pierce, Kevin Garnett, and Ray Allen beat the Lakers in the 2008 Finals were not even born in the 1980s! Still, they celebrated Boston's 17th NBA Championship with all the passion of generations past.

LEFT: Larry Bird pulls up for a jump shot during the 1986 NBA Finals.
ABOVE: Paul Pierce is the picture of joy after leading the Celtics to their 17th league title.

Go-To Guys

To be a true star in the NBA, you need more than a great shot. You have to be a "go-to guy"—someone teammates trust to make the winning play when the seconds are ticking away in a big game. Celtics fans have had a lot to cheer about over the years, including these great stars …

THE PIONEERS

BOB COUSY   6´ 1˝ Guard

• BORN: 8/9/1928   • PLAYED FOR TEAM: 1950–51 TO 1962–63

Bob Cousy was the point guard for six championship teams in Boston. His

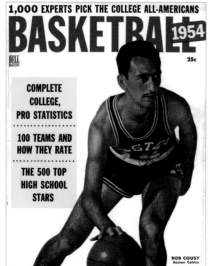

tricky dribbling and passing fueled the Celtics' offense. Cousy was an NBA All-Star 13 times.

BILL SHARMAN   6´ 1˝ Guard

• BORN: 5/25/1926

• PLAYED FOR TEAM: 1951–52 TO 1960–61

Bill Sharman believed that practice made perfect. He was not only one of the NBA's best shooters, he was probably the most physically fit player in the league. Sharman led the NBA in free-throw shooting seven times.

TOM HEINSOHN   6´ 7˝ Forward

• BORN: 8/26/1934   • PLAYED FOR TEAM: 1956–57 TO 1964–65

Tom Heinsohn was a smart, *competitive* player who was a great shooter and rebounder for the Celtics in the 1950s and 1960s. Later in the 1970s, he coached the team to two championships.

BILL RUSSELL   6´ 9˝ Center

• BORN: 2/12/1934   • PLAYED FOR TEAM: 1956–57 TO 1968–69

Bill Russell was the heart of 11 championship teams. He was the NBA MVP five times from 1958 to 1965, and also coached the Celtics to league titles in 1968 and 1969. Russell averaged at least 20 rebounds a game 10 seasons in a row.

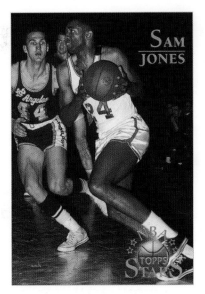

SAM JONES   6´ 4˝ Guard

• BORN: 6/24/1933

• PLAYED FOR TEAM: 1957–58 TO 1968–69

A great team needs a **clutch** go-to scorer. During the 1960s, Sam Jones was that player for Boston. Jones was the first Celtic to score 2,000 points in a season. His specialty was the bank shot.

JOHN HAVLICEK   6´ 5˝ Forward/Guard

• BORN: 4/8/1940   • PLAYED FOR TEAM: 1962–63 TO 1977–78

Most players slow down at age 30, but not John Havlicek. In the early 1970s, he was the NBA's best **all-around** forward. Havlicek led the Celtics back to the top of the basketball world in 1974 and 1976.

LEFT: Bob Cousy   **ABOVE**: Sam Jones

JO JO WHITE   6′ 3″ **Guard**

- BORN: 11/16/1946
- PLAYED FOR TEAM: 1969–70 TO 1978–79

There were many flashy and exciting guards in the NBA during the 1970s. Jo Jo White got the job done with quiet grace and class. He was the MVP of the 1976 NBA Finals.

DAVE COWENS   6′ 9″ **Center**

- BORN: 10/25/1948
- PLAYED FOR TEAM: 1970–71 TO 1979–80

Dave Cowens looked small compared to other NBA centers of his day. But no one could match his will to win. Cowens was the league MVP in 1972–73. He finished his career with more than 10,000 rebounds.

LARRY BIRD   6′ 9″ **Forward**

- BORN: 12/7/1956   • PLAYED FOR TEAM: 1979–80 TO 1991–92

Larry Bird did not look like a superstar, but he played like one. Bird was at his best in close games and often hit **3-point shots** with the clock winding down. He was voted the 1979–80 **Rookie of the Year** and was named the NBA MVP three seasons in a row.

ABOVE: Jo Jo White   **RIGHT**: Kevin Garnett

KEVIN McHALE   6´ 10˝ Forward

- BORN: 12/19/1957
- PLAYED FOR TEAM: 1980–81 TO 1992–93

Boston's opponents never figured out how to deal with Kevin McHale. If they guarded him with a center, then Robert Parish would be open. If they guarded McHale with a forward, he would shoot and rebound right over his opponent. In 1996, McHale was voted one of the top 50 players in NBA history.

PAUL PIERCE   6´ 6˝ Forward

- BORN: 10/13/1977
- FIRST SEASON WITH TEAM: 1998–99

Few players have ever been harder to stop than Paul Pierce. From the moment he joined the Celtics, he proved he could score from anywhere on the court. Pierce was named MVP of the 2008 NBA Finals.

KEVIN GARNETT   6´ 11˝ Forward

- BORN: 5/19/1976
- FIRST SEASON WITH TEAM: 2007–08

Kevin Garnett entered the NBA in 1995 as a teenager. When he joined the Celtics 12 years later, he gave the team a high-energy big man, just like they had in the 1960s and 1970s. Along with Ray Allen, Garnett helped Boston become a championship team.

On the Sidelines

The Celtics have had many excellent coaches over the years, including Tom Heinsohn, Bill Fitch, K.C. Jones, Chris Ford, and Rick Pitino. All of them worked for the greatest coach of all, Red Auerbach. He joined the Celtics in 1950–51. Over the next 16 years with Auerbach in charge, the team never had a losing record.

Auerbach created basketball's greatest winning machine. By combining the different skills of his players, he was able to get the very best out of each of them. In the 10 years from 1957 to 1966, Boston won the NBA crown nine times. When Auerbach retired from coaching, he stayed with the Celtics to run the team. His star center, Bill Russell, then became Boston's player-coach. The Celtics won two more championships with Russell in charge.

Auerbach watched proudly from the stands as his team won five more championships in the 1970s and 1980s. He passed away before the Celtics won it all again in 2008. There is no doubt Auerbach would have been proud of Boston's coach that year. Doc Rivers was a former NBA All-Star who asked his players to play **team basketball**. That was exactly the way Auerbach coached.

Larry Bird and Red Auerbach celebrate Boston's championship in 1985–86.

One Great Day

The Celtics have enjoyed many **unforgettable** victories during the NBA Finals. However, their greatest triumph might have come in the second round of the 1965 **postseason**. Boston played the Philadelphia 76ers. Earlier in the year, the 76ers had traded for Wilt Chamberlain. He and Bill Russell were famous for their one-on-one

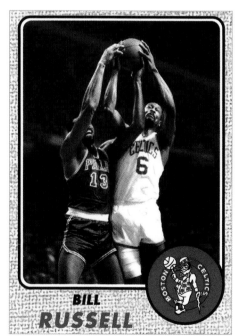

BILL
RUSSELL

battles. Chamberlain often scored more points and grabbed more rebounds, but Russell usually found a way to win. Now Chamberlain had a chance to keep Boston from going to the NBA Finals for the first time in nine years.

The Celtics won three games at home, and so did the 76ers. Game 7 was played in the Boston Garden. The fans cheered as the Celtics opened up an 18-point lead early in the game. The 76ers did not give up. They cut Boston's lead to 110–109 with five seconds left to play.

Russell **inbounded** the ball from the **baseline** under Boston's basket. His pass hit a wire holding up the backboard. The 76ers were awarded the ball with time left to make the winning shot. The Celtics called a timeout.

"Man, somebody bail me out!" said an embarrassed Russell.

The Celtics knew that the 76ers would try to get the ball to Chamberlain. He was having a great game and had just dunked over Russell. Since Chamberlain was a poor free throw shooter, Boston planned to foul him as soon as he had the ball.

The 76ers knew this, too. Instead, they set up a play to create an open shot for Chet Walker. As Philadelphia's Hal Greer prepared to pass to Walker, John Havlicek realized the ball was not going to Chamberlain. He leaped high in the air and tipped the pass before Walker could reach it. Sam Jones of the Celtics grabbed the ball and threw it back to Havlicek. As the final buzzer sounded, Boston announcer Johnny Most screamed again and again, "Havlicek stole the ball!"

The first player to hug Havlicek was Russell. All the big center could say was "Thank you."

LEFT: A trading card shows Wilt Chamberlain and Bill Russell battling for a loose ball.   **ABOVE**: John Havlicek, the hero of the playoff series against the Philadelphia 76ers.

Legend Has It

Was Bill Russell the first African-American coach of a major sports team?

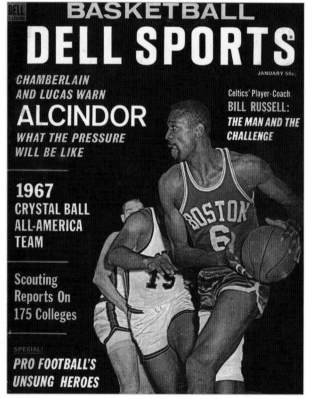

LEGEND HAS IT that he was. In 1966, Red Auerbach made his 32-year-old center a player-coach. The NBA was not only a "major" league at this time, the Celtics were the league's most famous team. The stubborn, super-competitive Russell had never coached before. Auerbach often joked that he chose the only coach besides himself that Russell would play for. Under their new coach, the Celtics won 60 games in 1966–67, but fell short of a championship. In each of the next two seasons, Russell led Boston to the NBA title.

ABOVE: A 1967 magazine explores Bill Russell's challenge as player-coach of the Celtics. **TOP RIGHT**: Paul Pierce dunks over Shaquille O'Neal during the 2004 All-Star Game. **BOTTOM RIGHT**: Tom Heinsohn, who was also known as "Ack-Ack."

Which Celtic got his nickname from a movie?

LEGEND HAS IT that Paul Pierce did. In *A Few Good Men*, Jack Nicholson's character delivers a famous line: "You can't handle the truth!" NBA All-Star Shaquille O'Neal often talked about how hard Pierce was to handle. O'Neal decided to give his buddy a nickname. The first thing that came to mind was—what else?—The Truth.

Which Celtic got his nickname from a gun?

LEGEND HAS IT that Tom Heinsohn did. Heinsohn's job on the Celtics was to shoot as often as possible. He reminded fans of the American anti-aircraft guns used in World War II to shoot at enemy planes. The sound those guns made was ack-ack-ack-ack-ack. Heinsohn's nickname was—you guessed it—Ack-Ack!

It Really Happened

Many times over their history, the Celtics have turned losses into wins with amazing plays. That is why Boston fans never give up. Even so, the situation seemed hopeless in Game 5 of the 1987 Eastern Conference Finals.

The Detroit Pistons were ahead 107–106 with only five seconds left. Their best player, Isiah Thomas, had the ball out of bounds. All he had to do was pass to a teammate, and the Pistons could let the clock tick away.

Larry Bird knew he had to make a steal. When Bird saw Thomas look at Bill Laimbeer, he sprinted in the big center's direction. Bird got there just in time to tip the ball away. But as he grabbed the ball at the sideline, he could not gain his balance. As Bird began to fall out of bounds, he saw a flash of white and green. It was Dennis Johnson. Bird fired the ball into the hands of his teammate.

"DJ" made an easy layup with the scoreboard reading 0:01. The Celtics won the game 108–107. The Pistons learned a hard lesson that day. Never count out the Celtics until there are three zeros on the clock!

Dennis Johnson and Larry Bird celebrate a win during the team's glory years in the 1980s. They worked together to produce one of Boston's most unforgettable baskets.

Team Spirit

No basketball team has better fans than the Celtics. The crowds at old Boston Garden wanted to win as badly as the players they rooted for. The arena used to shake when the fans rose to their feet and cheered their loudest. The Celtics almost never lost a Game 7 when they played in front of their fans. The same is true today. Boston fans love the Celtics, and they are not shy about showing it.

The Celtics have one of the NBA's most well-known *mascots*, Lucky the Leprechaun. In the old days, Lucky would roam the court and get the fans excited. Now Lucky is a slam-dunking acrobatic mascot.

Lucky is not alone when it comes to entertaining the fans. The team has lots of things for kids to do during games and holds fun contests at halftime. In 2006, the Celtics Dancers took the floor for the first time. Boston had never had a dance team before. It has become one of the most popular in the NBA.

Fans greet Paul Pierce after the Celtics clinch the 2008 NBA Championship.

Timeline

The basketball season is played from October through June. That means each season takes place at the end of one year and the beginning of the next. In this timeline, the accomplishments of the Celtics are shown by season.

1946–47
The Celtics play their first season.

1957–58
Bill Russell gets 40 rebounds in a playoff game.

1956–57
The Celtics win their first championship.

1959–60
Bob Cousy leads the NBA in **assists** for the eighth year in a row.

1966–67
Bill Russell is named coach of the Celtics.

Bob
Cousy

Bill
Russell

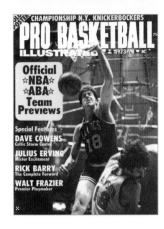

Dave
Cowens

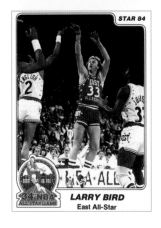

Larry
Bird

1972–73
Dave Cowens is
named NBA MVP.

1985–86
Larry Bird is named
NBA MVP for the
third year in a row.

2001–02
Antoine Walker
leads the NBA in
minutes played.

1980–81
The Celtics win
their 14th NBA
Championship.

1995–96
Dino Radja leads
the team in scoring
and rebounds.

2007–08
The Celtics are
NBA champions
for the 17th time.

Cedric Maxwell,
a star for the
1981 champs.

Doc Rivers, coach
of the 2008
champs.

Fun Facts

GOING GREEN

Newcomers Kevin Garnett, Ray Allen, and Sam Cassell helped the Celtics go from a 24–58 record in 2006–07 to a 66–16 record in 2007–08. No team had ever improved by 42 wins in one year.

SHARMAN on Basketball Shooting

By Bill Sharman

Bill Sharman, who ranks eighth in all-time NBA scoring, hitting 42% of his field goals and 88% of his free throws . . . reveals all his know-how in the only complete guide to basketball shooting — fundamentals, footwork, timing, faking — plus scores of drills that develop leading scorers in any league.

THE WRITE STUFF

Bill Sharman was an expert on the art of shooting. After his playing days with the Celtics, he wrote a 222-page book on the subject!

MAKING A POINT

The Celtics have won each of their championships playing unselfish basketball. That is one reason why no Celtic has ever won an NBA scoring championship.

HAIL TO THE CHIEF

During the 1980s, Robert Parish led the Celtics in rebounds eight years and was an All-Star seven times. When he retired from the NBA, "The Chief" had played 21 seasons—more than anyone in history.

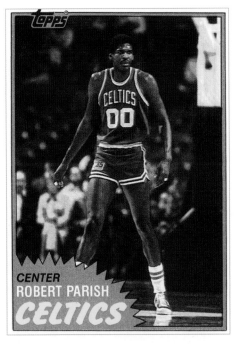

CLASH OF THE TITANS

During the 1960s, the rivalry between Bill Russell and Wilt Chamberlain was one of the most exciting in sports. The NBA scheduled their games to be on national television as often as possible. Millions of people became lifelong fans watching the two amazing centers play.

BIRD CALL

Everyone called Larry Bird Boston's top player during the 1980s. Did he agree? Bird claims that defensive star Dennis Johnson was the best he ever played with.

LEFT: Bill Sharman's book on shooting.
ABOVE: Robert Parish, whose nickname was "The Chief."

Talking Hoops

"The Celtics aren't a team. They're a way of life."
—*Red Auerbach, on Boston's bond with its fans*

"Our practices were fierce because the guys on the bench wanted to play. They knew they were good enough to start on other teams."
—*Tom "Satch" Sanders, on the Celtics of the 1960s*

"Star players have an enormous responsibility beyond their statistics—the responsibility to pick up their team and carry it. You have to do this to win championships."
—*Bill Russell, on the importance of teamwork*

"Who cares who gets the last shot or scores the most points? Who cares who gets the credit? If we win, we're all winners."

—Paul Pierce, on sharing the ball with his teammates

"Approach each practice shot as if you were behind with three seconds left to play. And never goof around in practice."

—Frank Ramsey, on the key to becoming a good pressure shooter

"I don't know if I practiced more than anybody, but I sure practiced enough."

—Larry Bird, on how he became a superstar

"That was the key to the Celtics' greatness—not getting on top, but making the sacrifices to stay there."

—Bob Cousy, on how Boston won 11 NBA titles in 13 years

LEFT: Tom Sanders and Bill Russell, two of Boston's leaders during the 1960s.   **ABOVE**: Frank Ramsey

For the Record

The great Celtics teams and players have left their marks on the record books. These are the "best of the best" …

CELTICS ACHIEVEMENTS

ACHIEVEMENT	SEASON	ACHIEVEMENT	SEASON
Eastern Division Champions	1956–57	Eastern Division Champions	1967–68
NBA Champions	1956–57	NBA Champions	1967–68
Eastern Division Champions	1957–58	Eastern Division Champions	1968–69
Eastern Division Champions	1958–59	NBA Champions	1968–69
NBA Champions	1958–59	Eastern Conference Champions	1973–74
Eastern Division Champions	1959–60	NBA Champions	1973–74
NBA Champions	1959–60	Eastern Conference Champions	1975–76
Eastern Division Champions	1960–61	NBA Champions	1975–76
NBA Champions	1960–61	Eastern Conference Champions	1980–81
Eastern Division Champions	1961–62	NBA Champions	1980–81
NBA Champions	1961–62	Eastern Conference Champions	1983–84
Eastern Division Champions	1962–63	NBA Champions	1983–84
NBA Champions	1962–63	Eastern Conference Champions	1984–85
Eastern Division Champions	1963–64	Eastern Conference Champions	1985–86
NBA Champions	1963–64	NBA Champions	1985–86
Eastern Division Champions	1964–65	Eastern Conference Champions	1986–87
NBA Champions	1964–65	Eastern Conference Champions	2007–08
Eastern Division Champions	1965–66	NBA Champions	2007–08
NBA Champions	1965–66		

Don Chaney, a key member of Boston's championship teams in 1968–69 and 1973–74.

CELTICS AWARD WINNERS

WINNER	AWARD	SEASON
Ed Macauley	All-Star Game MVP	1950–51
Bob Cousy	All-Star Game MVP	1953–54
Bill Sharman	All-Star Game MVP	1954–55
Bob Cousy	All-Star Game MVP	1956–57
Bob Cousy	Most Valuable Player	1956–57
Tom Heinsohn	Rookie of the Year	1956–57
Bill Russell	Most Valuable Player	1957–58
Bill Russell	Most Valuable Player	1960–61
Bill Russell	Most Valuable Player	1961–62
Bill Russell	All-Star Game MVP	1962–63
Bill Russell	Most Valuable Player	1962–63
Bill Russell	Most Valuable Player	1964–65
Red Auerbach	Coach of the Year	1964–65
Dave Cowens	co-Rookie of the Year	1970–71
Dave Cowens	All-Star Game MVP	1972–73
Dave Cowens	Most Valuable Player	1972–73
Tom Heinsohn	Coach of the Year	1972–73
John Havlicek	NBA Finals MVP	1973–74
Jo Jo White	NBA Finals MVP	1975–76
Bill Fitch	Coach of the Year	1979–80
Larry Bird	Rookie of the Year	1979–80
Nate Archibald	All-Star Game MVP	1980–81
Cedric Maxwell	NBA Finals MVP	1980–81
Larry Bird	All-Star Game MVP	1981–82
Kevin McHale	Sixth Man Award	1983–84
Larry Bird	Most Valuable Player	1983–84
Larry Bird	NBA Finals MVP	1983–84
Kevin McHale	Sixth Man Award*	1984–85
Larry Bird	Most Valuable Player	1984–85
Larry Bird	3-Point Shootout Champion	1985–86
Bill Walton	Sixth Man Award	1985–86
Larry Bird	Most Valuable Player	1985–86
Larry Bird	NBA Finals MVP	1985–86
Larry Bird	3-Point Shootout Champion	1986–87
Larry Bird	3-Point Shootout Champion	1987–88
Dee Brown	Slam Dunk Champion	1990–91
Gerald Green	Slam Dunk Champion	2006–07
Kevin Garnett	Defensive Player of the Year	2007–08
Paul Pierce	NBA Finals MVP	2007–08

* *The Sixth Man Award is given to the league's best substitute player.*

TOP: Don Nelson, a star for the Celtics in the 1960s and 1970s. **ABOVE**: Nate Archibald, MVP of the 1981 All-Star Game.

Pinpoints

The history of a basketball team is made up of many smaller stories. These stories take place all over the map—not just in the city a team calls "home." Match the push-pins on these maps to the Team Facts and you will begin to see the story of the Celtics unfold!

TEAM FACTS

1 Boston, Massachusetts—*The Celtics have played here since the 1946–47 season.*

2 Union City, New Jersey—*Tom Heinsohn was born here.*

3 Baltimore, Maryland—*Reggie Lewis was born here.*

4 West Baden Springs, Indiana—*Larry Bird was born here.*

5 Chicago, Illinois—*Antoine Walker was born here.*

6 Newport, Kentucky—*Dave Cowens was born here.*

7 Middleton, Tennessee—*Bailey Howell was born here.*

8 Monroe, Louisiana—*Bill Russell was born here.*

9 Abilene, Texas—*Bill Sharman was born here.*

10 Eugene, Oregon—*Danny Ainge was born here.*

11 San Pedro, California—*Dennis Johnson was born here.*

12 Split, Croatia—*Dino Radja was born here.*

Larry Bird

Play Ball

Basketball is a sport played by two teams of five players. NBA games have four 12-minute quarters—48 minutes in all—and the team that scores the most points when time has run out is the winner. Most baskets count for two points. Players who make shots from beyond the three-point line receive an extra point. Baskets made from the free-throw line count for one point. Free throws are penalty shots awarded to a team, usually after an opponent has committed a foul. A foul is called when one player makes hard contact with another.

Players can move around all they want, but the player with the ball cannot. He must bounce the ball with one hand or the other (but never both) in order to go from one part of the court to another. As long as he keeps "dribbling," he can keep moving.

In the NBA, teams must attempt a shot every 24 seconds, so there is little time to waste. The job of the defense is to make it as difficult as possible to take a good shot—and to grab the ball if the other team shoots and misses.

This may sound simple, but anyone who has played the game knows that basketball can be very complicated. Every player on the court has a job to do. Different players have different strengths and weaknesses. The coach must mix these players in just the right way, and teach them to work together as one.

The more you play and watch basketball, the more "little things" you are likely to notice. The next time you are at a game, look for these plays:

PLAY LIST

ALLEY-OOP—A play where the passer throws the ball just to the side of the rim—so a teammate can catch it and dunk in one motion.

BACK-DOOR PLAY—A play where the passer waits for his teammate to fake the defender away from the basket—then throws him the ball when he cuts back toward the basket.

KICK-OUT—A play where the ball-handler waits for the defense to surround him—then quickly passes to a teammate who is open for an outside shot. The ball is not really kicked in this play; the term comes from the action of pinball machines.

NO-LOOK PASS—A play where the passer fools a defender (with his eyes) into covering one teammate—then suddenly passes to another without looking.

PICK-AND-ROLL—A play where one teammate blocks or "picks off" another's defender with his body—then cuts to the basket for a pass in the confusion.

Glossary

BASKETBALL WORDS TO KNOW

3-POINT SHOTS—Baskets made from behind the 3-point line.

ALL-AROUND—Good at all parts of the game.

ALL-STARS—Players selected to play in the annual All-Star Game.

ASSISTS—Passes that lead to successful shots.

BASELINE—The line that runs behind the basket, from one corner of the court to the other.

CLUTCH—Able to perform well under pressure.

CONFERENCE SEMIFINALS—The playoff series that decide which teams move on to the conference finals.

DRAFT PICKS—College players selected or "drafted" by NBA teams each summer.

EASTERN CONFERENCE FINALS—The playoff series that determines which team from the East will play the best team from the West for the NBA Championship.

FAST BREAK—An offensive play in which the team with the ball rushes down the court to take a shot.

HALL OF FAMERS—Players voted into the Hall of Fame, the museum in Springfield, Massachusetts, where basketball's greatest stars are honored.

INBOUNDED—Passed the ball to a teammate from out of bounds after a stoppage in play.

MOST VALUABLE PLAYER (MVP)—The award given each year to the league's best player; also given to the best player in the league finals and All-Star Game.

NATIONAL BASKETBALL ASSOCIATION (NBA)—The professional league that has been operating since 1946–47.

NBA FINALS—The playoff series that decides the champion of the league.

OVERTIMES—Extra periods played when a game is tied after 48 minutes.

PLAYER-COACH—A person who plays for a team and coaches it at the same time.

PLAYOFFS—The games played after the season to determine the league champion.

POSTSEASON—Another term for playoffs.

PROFESSIONAL—A player or team that plays a sport for money. College players are not paid, so they are considered "amateurs."

ROLE PLAYERS—People who are asked to do specific things when they are in a game.

ROOKIE OF THE YEAR—The annual award given to the league's best first-year player.

ROSTER—The list of players on a team.

TEAM BASKETBALL—A style of play that involves everyone on the court instead of just one or two stars.

VETERANS—Players with great experience.

OTHER WORDS TO KNOW

CENTURY—A period of 100 years.

COMPETITIVE—Having a strong desire to win.

DECADES—Periods of 10 years; also specific periods, such as the 1950s.

FEROCIOUS—Extremely intense.

GENERATION—A period of years roughly equal to the time it takes for a person to be born, grow up, and have children.

LOGO—A symbol or design that represents a company or team.

MASCOTS—Animals or people believed to bring a group good luck.

POTENTIAL—Ability to become better.

RIVALRY—An extremely emotional competition.

SATIN—A smooth, shiny fabric.

SYMBOL—Something that represents a thought or idea.

SYNTHETIC—Made in a laboratory, not in nature.

SYSTEM—An organized plan for success.

TRADITION—A belief or custom that is handed down from generation to generation.

UNFORGETTABLE—Memorable and amazing.

Places to Go

ON THE ROAD

BOSTON CELTICS
1 Fleetcenter Place
Boston, Massachusettts 02114
(866) 4CELTIX

NAISMITH MEMORIAL BASKETBALL HALL OF FAME
1000 West Columbus Avenue
Springfield, Massachusetts 01105
(877) 4HOOPLA

ON THE WEB

THE NATIONAL BASKETBALL ASSOCIATION   www.nba.com
   • *Learn more about the league's teams, players, and history*

THE BOSTON CELTICS   www.nba.com/celtics
   • *Learn more about the Celtics*

THE BASKETBALL HALL OF FAME   www.hoophall.com
   • *Learn more about history's greatest players*

ON THE BOOKSHELF

To learn more about the sport of basketball, look for these books at your library or bookstore:

   • Hareas, John. *Basketball*. New York, New York: DK, 2005.

   • Hughes, Morgan. *Basketball*. Vero Beach, Florida: Rourke Publishing, 2005.

   • Thomas, Keltie. *How Basketball Works*. Berkeley, California: Maple Tree Press, distributed through Publishers Group West, 2005.

Index

PAGE NUMBERS IN **BOLD** REFER TO ILLUSTRATIONS.

Abdul-Jabbar, Kareem 17
Ainge, Danny 9, 43
Allen, Ray **4**, **10**, 11, **15**, 19, 23, 36,
Archibald, Nate 9, 41, **41**
Auerbach, Red 6, **6**, 7, 14, 16, **24**, 25, 28, 38, 41
Auerbach, Zang 14
Bias, Len 9
Bird, Larry **8**, 9, 18, **18**, 19, 22, **24**, 30, **31**, 35, **35**, 37, 39, 41, 43, **43**
Brown, Dee 41
Brown, Walter 6
Carr, M.L. 9
Cassell, Sam 36
Chamberlain, Wilt 26, **26**, 27, 37
Chaney, Don **40**
Cousy, Bob 6, 7, **7**, 16, **16**, 20, **20**, 34, **34**, 39, 41
Cowens, Dave 7, 17, 22, 35, **35**, 41, 43
Fitch, Bill 25, 41
Ford, Chris 25
Garnett, Kevin **4**, **10**, 11, 19, 23, **23**, 36, 41
Green, Gerald 41
Greer, Hal 27
Havlicek, John 7, 17, 21, 27, **27**, 41
Heinsohn, Tom 7, **7**, 16, 21, 25, 29, **29**, 41, 43
Henderson, Gerald 9
Howell, Bailey 7, 43
Johnson, Dennis 9, 30, **31**, 37, 43

Johnson, Magic **8**, 19
Jones, K.C. 25
Jones, Sam 7, 21, **21**, 27
Laimbeer, Bill 30
Lewis, Reggie 9, **9**, 43
Loscutoff, Jim 16
Macauley, Ed 6, 41
Maxwell, Cedric 9, 18, **35**, 41
McHale, Kevin 9, 18, 23, 41
Most, Johnny 27
Nelson, Don **41**
Nicholson, Jack 29
O'Neal, Shaquille 29, **29**
Parish, Robert 9, 18, 23, 37, **37**
Phillip, Andy 16
Pierce, Paul **4**, 9, **10**, 11, 19, **19**, 23, 29, **29**, **32**, 39, 41
Pitino, Rick 25
Posey, James **4**
Radja, Dino 35, 43
Ramsey, Frank 7, 16, 39, **39**
Rivers, Doc 25, **35**
Russell, Bill 7, **7**, 16, 17, 21, 25, 26, **26**, 27, 28, **28**, 34, **34**, 37, 38, **38**, 41, 43
Sanders, Tom "Satch" 38, **38**
Sharman, Bill 7, **14**, 16, 20, 36, **36**, 41, 43
Silas, Paul 7
Thomas, Isiah 30
Walker, Antoine 9, 11, 35, 43
Walker, Chet 27
Walton, Bill 9, 41
White, Jo Jo 7, 17, 22, **22**, 41

The Team

MARK STEWART has written more than 20 books on basketball, and over 100 sports books for kids. He grew up in New York City during the 1960s rooting for the Knicks and Nets, and now takes his two daughters, Mariah and Rachel, to watch them play. Mark comes from a family of writers. His grandfather was Sunday Editor of *The New York Times* and his mother was Articles Editor of *The Ladies Home Journal* and *McCall's*. Mark has profiled hundreds of athletes over the last 20 years. He has also written several books about his native New York, and New Jersey, his home today. Mark is a graduate of Duke University, with a degree in history. He lives with his daughters and wife, Sarah, overlooking Sandy Hook, New Jersey.

MATT ZEYSING is the resident historian at the Basketball Hall of Fame in Springfield, Massachusetts. His research interests include the origins of the game of basketball, the development of professional basketball in the first half of the twentieth century, and the culture and meaning of basketball in American society.